THE TEN TALES

The Ten Tales

DANIEL DANIELSON

Bel Books

Contents

1	First and Foremost..	1
2	The Naughty Librarian..	7
3	TP..	17
4	French Cuisine..	19
5	Short Little One..	31
6	Pick Up Styx..	37
7	Seventh Heaven..	39
8	Big Bertha..	44
9	Doing Time..	52
10	Never Again..	55

Chapter 1

First and Foremost..

In the 33 years I've been alive, I've slept with a total of 10 chicks in my life,
(technically 11)..

Here are their tales..

..dunk dung..

I met Laura at school and we hit it off straight away. Wasn't long before we hooked up at a disco and I asked her out. I'd always had girlfriends through school, but this was different. She was my first love. Funny how when you're younger you think you know love. Until you do haha..

I left home in Tamworth for her. Packed a spare pair of clothes in my school bag and got a taxi out to Manilla, where I was graciously taken in by her family.

When I was 17 a got us a place at a share house. It was a mix match of weirdos really, but it was our own space.

I left school in year 11 and started working full time as a brickies laborer. I busted my guts man for $10 a fucking hour, cash, plus my dole so it worked at the time for what I wanted.

At 18 I got us a flat, owned by one of my teachers and footy coach.
I filled it full of furniture.
I filled it full of appliances.
I filled it full of food.
I filled it full of smokes, weed, and alcohol.
And I filled it full of love..

Laura didn't need to spend a cent while we were there. She was my girl and I saw it as my role to provide for her. And I was quite stubborn and proud about it too..

I paid the rent.
I paid the bills.
I bought the food.
I paid for the drugs.

And she betrayed me..

I gave her everything man. Mind, Body, and Soul.. I've always been very sensitive. I don't mean emotional. I mean I have always had keen sensors.

I knew something was up. I could feel it in my bones as they say.
After bugging her for a while she spat it out..

"I had sex with Slade."

I lost control, and in hot blood, I smacked her with the back of my hand in the mouth. .

Fuck. Immediately I collapsed on the bed and started balling my eyes out, overwhelmed with the shame of what I had just done. I haven't cried that many times in my life, but that was definitely one of them.

Laura instantly pounced on my back to console me.

"It's Ok" she kept saying, "I'm sorry, It's not your fault."

I was a mess. Without a doubt my rock bottom. I've never felt as bad as I did that day again. Word.

And just then, in our finest hour, a knock at the door..

It was her step-mum, who after helping us so much was a custom to coming straight in after announcing herself.

I have never in my life seen that girl so scared. She picked me up and got me together. Dried my eyes and begged her guts outs for me not to say anything.. Because she knew just as well as everyone else in the family that that was very out of character for me, and the first thing they would ask is why..

And her step-mum knew firsthand how much effort I put into that relationship, as she was the one driving the ute when I got the flat. She saw me at work and kept the kitty while we saved up for the bond and stuff. My boss always paid me in hundred dollar notes and it was full of them.

No good. I told her straight away what had just happened. And on second glance she notice that Laura had a bit of a swollen lip. She sat with us and talked for a while. I'm sure she could feel me tearing myself apart.

She suggested that I go up to the hospital with her and speak to a mental health professional, which I did and took very seriously..

No charges were ever laid and we stayed together for a while after that. I woke up on my 19th birthday and finally found the strength to get away.
In full circle, I packed a bag of clothes and pissed off back to my Mums' house. Where once again I balled my eyes out..

We hooked up a few times after that, at her invitation mind you. So she couldn't have been hating on me that much at the time. But I can understand where some confusion may lie..

Laura fucking lied about it. She exaggerated the fuck out of it to make herself more interesting and milked the shit out of it to get a scholarship. She secured funding for her art degree that had been allocated for women that had survived domestic violence and abusive relationships and has been singing the same tune ever since..

But good on her I say. Truly. She was going nowhere with me Joe. She never would have achieved any of that had she still been with me. I'm a Bong Lord that lives my life a quarter mile at a time. Day by day by day by day. Up until recently, I've never much considered my future. I have seen some of her accomplishments on her sister's FB, and I'm not gonna lie. There is a part of me that's proud of her..

And obviously, that's not all that happened. We were together for 3 years mind you. We lost our virginity to each other under the pitter-patter of light rain on a tin roof. The first year was a bit rough as we ironed out the kinks of doing life with a partner, and the last year was even rougher..

But that year in the middle contains some of the fondest memories of my life, full of restaurants and horse and carriage rides. Full of joy and the warmth of another person that wants to be there..

She will always be my first, and you'd have to be pretty thick to deny maths. Speaking of which..

Chapter 2

The Naughty Librarian..

I never got with anyone for almost 18 months after that. My fucking heart was broken hey..

After being homeless for a while, I ended up at Doyle Court, with all the other miserable homeless cunts. I was sitting there wallowing in self-pity one day when the mail slipped under my door. Amongst it was a flyer for the Tafe's open day. And it was right then, and only had about an hour left. Snap decision got off my ass and walked up there. Signed up for the TPC, Tertiary Preparation Certificate, which is the HSC equivalent.

Started a couple of weeks later and ran into my little sister in the hall, dope! She was doing her year 10 a few classrooms down and I hadn't seen her for a couple of years now. I was dope, seeing her and being alive again and all that jazz.

We went to the canteen for lunch that day and I noticed this chick that worked in the little shop selling books, calculators, and shit. Quite shamelessly we immediately started eye fucking the shit out of each other. Oh, gee I wanted her. In my mind, she was a librarian and a little minx at that.

In hindsight, I should have just walked in there and bought a pen or something hey. But an opportunity did present itself in a short time. She was rounding the heads of student faculties for a team bonding, skill-building, and kayaking-type excursion. All paid for by the Tafe. You had me at paid for. So I invented my own title, Head of Sports haha, and tagged along. PS Tafe has no sport. Not even a handball team lol..

Darcy was her name, and I was drawn to her hey. And her to me. She thought it was hilarious that I was the Head of Sports, and was pretty happy that I was coming. And hopefully, she guessed right, as having an opportunity to meet her was definitely part of the reason I jumped on board. We did all kinds of workshops and activities, including archery, a mechanical bull, and other cool shit. I always sat next to her when we had meals and really enjoyed talking to her hey.

We were having lunch one day while some people were having a go at each other gladiator style in the background. They had a balance beam set up and those poles with foam on the ends they use on the show.

Everyone was enjoying themselves until all of a sudden the room changed, hard. I turned around to see why, and it was because there was a guy and a chick on the beam, and he was wailing her hey. Didn't hold back one bit my man, was straight up feeding it to her hey, fuck..

He knocked her off the beam and onto the floor, after rattling her with a hard right, and I jumped straight up, fuck it. As I was heading over there, I noticed as she got up, she had a huge smile on her face. She gave me her weapon and said;

"It's OK, I told him to do it and not to hold back."

Fair enough, honestly. But he could have dialed it back a bit though shit. Just then he went to walk past me, looking for whoever was up next. I put my hand on his chest, stopping him dead in his tracks, and told him to;

"Get back on the fucking beam."

The tension was palpable. The room changed again, but this time it was buzzing full of electricity. We hopped up facing each other and I asked;

"You Ready?"

He got halfway through saying "Y" when I knocked his lips back inside his face. Fuck I Ca-racked him hey.

And the crowd went wild..

He fought back a bit after that, but I gave him a good little beating, and to his credit, he took a bit before conceding the fight and stepped off. I shook his hand after and told him to take it a bit easier on the girls. He agreed and told me that she told him to do it. Which I knew already but still I said;

"You didn't have to go that hard.."

I went and sat back down next to Darcy who I could tell was moister than an oyster. Preach.

I kept feigning ignorance even though I wanted her. I'm kinda broken, which makes things difficult hey.

When we got back from the trip, as we all got off the bus, she pulled me aside and asked if I wanted a lift home. I knew what she meant but my place was a mess and I piked it. I told her I only live a couple of blocks from there and was all good.

I saw her again on Thursday at the end of lunch. She came up and asked why I "always have lunch with Jenny', and if she was my 'girlfriend or something?'

I told her that she is my little sister and we always have lunch together. Once again she lit up like the Forth of July, so fuck it, I just asked her.

"What are you doing tomorrow?"

"Working again. Or do you mean for lunch?"

"Na, I mean after work.."

She came around Friday arvo with a liter of Bundy and a fifty of yarndii. Music to my soul. Pretty cool chick man. We talked for hours. I purposely kept it clean and allowed all the sexual tension to build in the background, while we pumped cones and sank the rum..

"Oh shit!" she said, "It's 11 o'clock, I should probably be getting home."

I walked up and got in her face and said;

"We should probably have some fun first."

Haha what a dumb thing to say, but it was all she was waiting for..

And I wasn't wrong about her hey. She may not have been a real librarian, but she was a real firecracker in the sack. Ahh man. Honestly, a lot of chicks think having sex is laying there and copping dick snot. It's not, that what you call getting fucked, sorry, not sorry. Sex is different, it's mutual. We started kissing hard and were naked by the time we hit the bed. As she sprawled out, I can quite clearly recall the realization I had at that moment. An epiphany if you will. Up until now, I was just a boy fooling around with a girl. Laura was two years young than me, about a foot shorter, and like most chicks shaved. But this was quite clearly a woman. She was hairy down there like she just don't care. And I love it. My natural instinct was to get a face full of it, in what can only be described as fast and furious oral sex. She grabbed me by the ears, pulled me up to her face, and invited me in. And she fucked me right back. For quite some time too, we went from the bed to the floor, to the couch, to the floor, and back again. We were even in the kitchen at one stage..

And after what felt like both an eternity, and an instant at the same time, we climaxed together and collapsed into a puddle of meat and sweat. I was beat hey, and so fucking dry. I asked her if she wanted a drink. Of course she did, she was in the same state I was. I managed to get up and walked over to the kitchen and when I opened the roller door my eyes nearly exploded right out of my head. It was broad fucking daylight..

I asked her, "Darcy what the fuck is the time?"

"Holy shit, it's 6 o'clock!!!"

Still my record 'til today, and I don't think I'll ever beat it either. I was 20 then, and that was a once in a lifetime effort hey..

"Ahh fuck. I gotta get home hey. Fuck.. Worst Mother of the Year Award."

Pause. Rewind. Replay..

Just as I thought, no previous mention of any kids. Ok, dropping bombs on the way out are we? That was in fact the second red flag, to tell the truth. The first in hindsight was thinking Jenny was my girlfriend.

"How many kids do you have?"

"Two little ones. It's OK, they are with their Dad."

'..'

"We are not together anymore, we're just both there for the kids for now."

"Yea it's all good. You better get back to them then."

"Can I see you again tonight?" She asked.

"How about tomorrow night.." I laughed.

She laughed too, kissed me, and took off. So did I. Straight to bed, and crashed hard..

When I woke up I was so fucking sore, I swear my legs had been ripped off and shoved back on. And the elastic on the front of my boxers was burning and cutting into me. I had a go at what was going on, and my pelvis was so bruised and swollen it looked like Shack's forehead..

Straight away I thought of her and what we did, then I remember thinking it was a good call on tomorrow night. Then I remembered she said she had kids. I didn't mind besides the fact she had kept it from me hey. I don't like that shit. We talked for hours before we talked for hours that night, and not one mention. Hmm..

She came around the next night with a 750ml Bundy and a stick. Massaged the Jesus out of my back and we had sex again. But normal sex this time. Not Hulk vs She-Hulk sex like the other night. I didn't have any moisturizer so she used my conditioner, and I still can't use Dove until this day. And that's fuct because I love that shit..

The next morning she sent me a message when she got home that said;

-I want to be your girl.-

And just then a demon crawled up from the pits of purgatory and screeched:

"RELATIONSHIP!!!!"

So, accordingly, I pooped my little panties. I soiled my tighty whities. And I made a Ca-Ca in my Boom-Boom..

After an awkward silence, she messaged back saying it was too much hey? And more messages ensued, lots of them actually. I didn't ignore her, just told her I'm not there yet and that I liked what we had. And the messages didn't stop. Crazy shit too. So I avoided her because she was clearly crazy.

Not kidding. A few days later she made my heart sink..

I wasn't going to the canteen anymore. Fuck that. I was sitting at a table just outside our classroom having lunch with a few people when I got a message from Tracy. Naming those few people I was having lunch with, and suggested I had moved on to one of them.

FUCKING SHAT MYSELF..

-:Lord God Baby Jesus. I know I haven't believed in you up until now, but I need you to do us a solid man. And maybe on the sly or something, could you whack this bitch with a lightning bolt, please? She has strayed from the flock and lost the plot. I'll go to church and plant trees and shit, just one teeny tiny little lightning bolt please??:-

Fuck me, man. She was straight-up stalking me. And then she started bailing chicks up at the Impy and accusing them of sleeping with me and shit. She was off her head, so I had to straighten her out, and never really saw her or heard from her again. And even though she was bat shit crazy, she did make a man of me..

Chapter 3

TP..

You may start to see a pattern emerging here. I'm afraid things are about to get a bit wild..

I was drinking with a few boys, Brother A, Brother D, and Brother J, at Doyle Court not long after that. There was this chick there I'll, Lady X, who was quite a promiscuous extravert. And even though she was flirting with everyone, she only had eyes for one of us, Brother A. At the end of the night, I was pretty burnt and went up to my unit and crashed. Well, I nearly crashed, when there was a knock at the door. It was Brother J. And Lady X? He simultaneously pushed passed me, pulled her in, closed the door, and said;

"Shhh.."

And who says men can't multitask? Anyone that knows Brother J, knows for a fact he was a playa. Not some buster that inspired to be, or tried to be, or wished they were. He was living it. "Hand to God", as they say. And as I say;

"He caught more tail than a fucking shrimp boat."

He didn't mess around either, took her from behind and pointed her face straight at my belt. In no time after that, he spun her around and we switched. Then he told me to take her into the kitchen because he had another chick he wanted to take into the bathroom waiting just outside. Cool dude this Brother J. I told ya. She was a bit more bashful and required privacy. So this cheeky bugger lined Lady X up for me, so he could use my washing machine with her. After they finished a load, she disappeared and the other two boys from before, Brother A and Brother D, came in. And Lady X thoroughly enjoyed all four of us. I'm talking spit roasts, DP, TP, and just all-out gangbang madness. It was a pretty fucking crazy night hey. But when in Rome, just go with it, fuck it..

Chapter 4

French Cuisine..

Not long after my 21st, I fuct right up, went on the run, and moved to Ipswich, QLD. It's a lot like Tamworth, just bigger. Tamworth's population is 77k, and Ipswich's is 233k, so about 3 times bigger. But the same kind of vibe hey. It's a city, but you can still run into people you know down the street. I guess being an outlaw kind of went to my head, because the next eight stories all took place over a twelve-month period..

I was staying with friends in Riverview when they told me about River Fire. A festival they have in Brisbane every year. So we got the train into the City, which is only about 35min, and got amongst it. After a bit of bar hopping, we tried to get into this one pub, couldn't tell you the name, in South Bank near the big Ferris Wheel. At this stage and was just me and my mate Jimmy. And I say we tried to get in, but really I mean, I tried to get in. Jimmy was right, but my license was expired and this one bouncer wouldn't let me go through. Fucker..

Jimmy said we should just go somewhere, else but I'm known to be quite a silly coont when I'm drunk haha. I told him;

"Na Unk, you go in and have a good night. I'll catch up with you later.."

Love you, Jimmy. Not knowing what was up, but clearly knowing something was up, he followed my lead and just went in. I like that shit. Full trust in a man, it's dope..

The pub in question had cut themselves out a nice slice of the strip with one of those Rent-a-Fence jobs. You know the tall metal cage-type portable fences with the big yellow weights down the bottom. Normally it must have been open-range drinking, but they had surrounded the beer garden from one end of the building to the other, leaving only one small opening. Creating, in theory, the only entry..

All I did was walk around the fence, to the other end of the pub, to where the fence started, or ended, depending on your philosophical view. Simply lifted the fence out of the yellow weight, swung it out a bit, stepped in, and put it back. There, a small, dead-end corridor was temporarily made by the building, the fence, and a feature garden, and was allocated the smoking area. But one dude saw me putting the fence back and yelled;

'HHHHEEEEEYYYYYYYY!!!!!!!!!!!!!!!!!!!'

And I said, "SSSHHH!!!!! Shut the fuck man. What are you doing?"

He said, 'Shit, sorry man, my bad, but that was awesome!'

"Yea alright buddy, cool. But take it easy, don't give me up hey?.."

As I walked past him, boom. This chick caught my eye, and I forgot all about Jimmy, the bouncer, the fence, and the dude. She had one side of her head shaved, just around her ear, exposing the tattoo of a vibrant, evergreen vine. It came up out of her shirt, crept up her neck, and twisted around the top of her ear. It was wicked..

But she had a bloke, or so I thought anyways. Nevertheless, I snapped out of it and went to find Jimmy. My man, he was just floating around the bar looking for me when I spotted him. I went up to him and he told me to find us a table while he grabbed a jug.

And just then, the heavens opened up, and some deity I'd never even heard of, dropped something and it landed right in front of me..

As far as I could see, was a sea, of tables occupardo. But smack bang center stage, front row was a tiny little empty table for two. I swooped in like a pa-terodactyl. And WHACK! As soon as I sat down, I was assaulted right in the face by a couple of young, hot lesbians. I noticed when I was looking for a table, that everyone was acting as if there was a movie playing behind or something. Except for those who were there with their wives or girlfriends, they were all staring at their shoelaces. But everyone else was watching this one chick, who had this other chick, pinned up against a wooden support beam, and was dry-humping the Christ out of her. Then, I shit you not, she slipped her hand down the front of her pants and started finger-blasting her right in front of everyone..

Jimmy got back with the jug, two glasses and sat down. I asked him;

"How do you like the seats?"

'Yea good one.'

"And what about the view?"

He turned around and saw what was going on and immediately stopped pouring the beers. The look on his face. And mine, and everyone else. All the other chicks were enjoying the show too. A few dirty birdies were even singing some shit out, lol. After the show was over and we were on our last beer, we went up the back for a smoke. That chick was still there, and so was the same guy, he was all up in her business just as he was before, so I assumed they were together.

She had a foreign accent, yum. I couldn't pick it at first, and she wasn't so easy as to divulge such personal information without a fight..

'I come from the land of wine and cheese..." she told me.

I do love a good riddle. Especially when the answer is, she was French!

"What happened to your husband?"

'Oh, he's not my husband.'

"Sorry, your boyfriend."

She shook her head.

"Fiancé?"

'That guy has been pestering me for over an hour now. I'm glad you came along. He took off after we started talking.'

So you're telling me, there's no goalie, and I have a penalty shot? Is that what you are saying to me? I have a genuine chance with a French chick. A sexy, cool as shit, French chick. Fuck yea let's roll. I asked her;

"What's up with the French kiss? I reckon that's kinda bullshit. People kiss like that all over the world."

She laughed and replied. 'True. But maybe the French invented it.'

Boom. Boom. Fair enough. "Maybe", she said. I like that. She didn't know, and made that clear. Love it. We kept talking until our glasses ran dry and I offered her another. She told me to be quick.

However, as I was working my way up the line, the bar started shutting down and the staff were shooing people out. FARRRK. In all the confusion I lost her, found Jimmy, and got herded out onto the street.

FARRRK. I felt like Jack from the Titanic sinking in the cold water. Jimmy offered me his condolences and we resorted to just getting the train back home..

But wham, out of nowhere, it was my Rose. But she wasn't like that silly bitch in the movie, she was more like;

"Look I have a door, jump on and let's get the fuck outta here."

She grabbed me by my jumper on the back of my arm and said;

'Hey! I thought I lost ya.'

"Well, that's coz you did. But then you found me.."

Sorry Jimmy.

'See ya tomorrow.' he said with a smile on his face, and without needing to hear a word from me, and then took off for the train station.

She said good night to Jimmy and saw him off. Then she stepped in nice and close to me, looked up with a smile, and said;

'You were asking about the French kiss before, but I want to know about the Aboriginal kiss...'

So I took my hoody off and kissed her. And it was good. She then suggested that we go to a hotel. I told you, some God somewhere threw me a bone hey..

She knew of one close called the Albatross, so we took a short train ride there and she acted like we were newlyweds the entire time.

'Why do you not like kissing me?' she asked at one stage.

"Na it's not that. It's just..'

'You are a little shy in public no?'

"Yea, that's all."

'OK, no worries. Just hold my hand OK?' she said and cuddled up to me. She was real cool about it, toned it back, and was very cute about it.

When we got there, we stopped in at a 7-11 across the road where she bought a packet of condoms, two 5hr energy shots, and a couple of tins of tuna. When we got to the lobby of the hotel, she insisted she paid for the room. Then she pounced on me as soon as the doors in the elevator closed and stopped before they reopened. She was so free and open, and it was dope. I felt a bit awkward about the whole situation, but she was so blasé. Very attractive..

When we got to the room, she gave me an energy drink and offered me a tin of tuna. I told her I was all good and drank the shot.

She told me in her sexy little French accent that she was really sorry, but also really hungry, haha.

"All good," I told her, I sat on the end of the bed and checked out the room a bit while she inhaled both tins with her back to me. Turned around and drank her shot and smiled, while staring me right in the eye. Thank you, Jesus. Maybe that's how it works. Maybe Jesus is just really backed up everyone's prayers and shit, and he finally got my message and was like:

-:Sh_t, F_ck, C_ck, C_nt! Sorry brother! I know it's a bit late now, but you really needed me to zap that bitch Darcy hey. Sorry brother. But ooowwweee, how's this! Right now, there is a lovely French chick in that pub that has always wanted to sleep with a black fulla. And for the fuck around, I'll even throw in some lesbians. Cool? Hey and don't be a stranger man. You can hit me up whenever. Peace!:-

She pounced on me again and pulled me back onto the bed. We rolled around for a while kissing until she was on top, and things got a bit more serious. Turns out my French Rose was hiding some pretty impressive tata's under her lady shirt. Apparently, the condoms were optional. She got straight to the point, rubbing me up against herself..

'Sorry,' she said, 'I like to rub it on my clit.'

No worries hey.

And we had a really good time. We both knew it was just us two, just for the night, and took advantage of every minute. I was on top when I got close, running my hands up her back, I nibbled my way up the vine on her neck and whispered;

"Is it alright if I come inside you?"

She answered by interlocking her ankles around my lower back and using it as leverage to pull us both closer together..

We woke up in the middle of the night and did it again. Woke up in the morning, and did it again. Then she suggested we had a shower, and did it again before we had to check out at 10. Honestly, I've been in Rome this whole time lady. I'm down. Nodding, I got out of the bed, and headed for the bathroom.

Now we were both starker's, so I wasn't expecting what happened next..

She went straight over to the curtains and casually went, "sssshhheeerrrttt.." Had a huge stretch and a yawn, in front of about 100 windows from the hotel across the road, and turned around looking like an angel. I on the other tucked tail and bolted into the bathroom. She looked at me confused and asked;

'What's wrong? You're beautiful!?'

Ahhh. Well, thanks love heart. Very sweat. But that's just not how I operate.   I jumped in the shower, she joined me and we did it again. Got dressed and she told me we still had half an hour, so we make the bed and sat there talking politics. Just kidding, we did it again. We checked out and then she told me she wanted to go to the chemist to get a morning-after pill, and asked if I would come. On the way, we passed a sushi joint and she went nuts, offering me some for brekkie but I don't really like it. When we got to the chemist, she told me just to hang around in the front end, while she went to the back counter. When she came back down, it was the first time I had her bashful.

'I don't want to ask but I haven't got much money left and I um..'

I just grabbed it and walked out the front. This chick was probably backpacking on a budget but still spoiled me all night, and then again in the morning. She met me a minute or so later and escorted me to the train station. Got my email address, gave me a huge kiss, and watched me leave. Wild dream come true..

And she actually did email me too. We kept in contact for a while, until she let me know found a bloke in NT and wished me well. Very cool chick..

Chapter 5

Short Little One..

Not long after that, the next weekend I think, I wandered into town drunk. Not far past The Squealing Pig, a popular watering hole in the main street of Ipswich. I noticed a chick on the pay phone. As I passed her she asked if I had a smoke. I reached into my pocket to grab my smokes, and she reached out and grabbed me on the fork..

'Oops!' she squeaked.

"That wasn't an accident.." I told her with a look of approval on my face.

She hung up the phone and took me by the hand. We went across the road to a little car park surrounded by a wooden picket fence at the top of town. Ipswich technically has two main streets. It spits into two one-way streets, divides for about eight blocks and then comes back together, where you can do a U-turn at either end and head back the other way..

It was about 2 or 3 in the morning so everything was closed, but it was the main street, and we were at a busy spot, as quite a few hooligans were zipping around. They probably couldn't see what we were doing, but then again maybe they could, and it was kinda hot. Jess was her name, and she was a short blonde cutie. As soon as we got there, she laid down on the bitumen and started taking off her pants. So I took mine off and laid on top of her. I won't lie, it lasted for roughly twelve and a half seconds but was one of the strongest orgasms I've ever had.. I looked at her as if to apologize and explain, but she said;

'Where have you been all my life?'

I'll take it. We got ourselves back together, had a little kiss, parted ways and we've never run into one another since..

Chapter 5.5: The Boy Who Cried Rape..

I don't really count this one, but, technically we did have sex. I was living in Brassall, a quiet suburb of Ipswich, with family at the time. I couldn't drink or smoke there, so I used to bugger off to the park down the road to get it on. I was there with this other guy I knew, Clarke, who I called Superman. It started to get dark when this chick came up with a little girl tagging along behind her and asked if she could have a drink with us. I spun out, but Clarke said;

'Yea, no worries.'

The little girl stayed back where she was, and the woman sat down. Yes, this is fast becoming shady af. But before I could open my mouth, this other bloke came up and asked her;

'Chrissy, are you coming home or not?'

'No. I'm having a drink with my new friends.'

'Come on baby.' And he took the little girl's hand and disappeared. Bazaar much. Wtf is going on here?

But before I could ask she told me that was her ex, and they are just together for their kid's sake. Ring any bells. I went for a walk to get more beers before the bottle-o closed, and to process the situation I guess. When I got back, it was dark dark, and I was a bit drunk. I sat down without noticing that those two were hooking up..

All I said was, "What's going on here?", and she turned around and started kissing me. Bad bitch. Real bad actually. She got up over my lap, grabbed me by the collar of my shirt, dragged me up to my feet and in towards her. Letting go of my shirt, she ran her hand down my chest, over my belt, and down my thigh. She then lifted up her skirt while hopping up on the table, where she pulled her knickers to the side. Fucken what?

I reached out to get a better sense of the situation but she beat me to it. I was unbuttoned, unzipped, and hard enough to cut stones, in less than seven seconds. She pulled my dick out with her right hand and took a handful of my ass cheek with her left. Rubbed it around on her pussy for a bit, and then pulled me into her. Taking another hand full of my ass, she used me like a thing for another seven seconds, then abruptly pushed me off and said;

'I wanna fuck on a bed! With a real mattress!' Then stood up and straightened herself out, like nothing had even happened..

What the shit?! I feel like that was rape hey. I think I got raped. I mean, an erection is kind of an involuntary action for the most part, but an action nonetheless. But I'm pretty sure that was a couple of paddle pop sticks a few rubber bands away from rape right? I didn't move a muscle, she literally used me..

Stupidly though, the night went on. After my raping, I rolled a smoke and Chrissy, noticing I only had about half a pouch, insisted she buy me a fresh one. Probably felt bad after raping me was my thought. She also bought two 3 racks of Jim Beam and gave us two each. We walked into the top of town and arrived at a familiar spot called The Squealing Pig. First time I had ever been in there actually. We went in and she asked what we were drinking. I was drinking beer, but I said;

"Rum. Bundaberg, Rum."

Then I went out to the smoking spot. She came out with a stubby of Bundy for me, a Jim Beam for Clarke, and a pink Cruiser for herself. Not sure why I walked all the way there and hung around to tell you the truth. Maybe because after she raped me I wanted the real thing, like some kind of Stockholm syndrome shit, I don't know. But when my drink was running low she offered me another and I said yes. Silly bugger..

While she was gone this young couple came out for a smoke and sat down next to me. We got to talking and all of a sudden, whack. This bitch walked up and full-slapped me hey. Crack, fuck she got me, it hurt too, I'm not going to lie. It came out of now where and fucking stung me hey. But before I could react, the little blonde chick I was talking to fully lunged at her, and grabbed her by the throat. Chrissy grabbed her by the hair, and they were into it, full ball for about 30 seconds before her bloke split it up. Crazy. Quite enjoyable, but crazy nonetheless. Even crazier, Chrissy goes off saying;

'I haven't been buying you drinks all night just to have you talking to this other bitch!'

I thought it was on again for sure. No. This little blonde chick fully sympathized with her, and replied;

'Ahh sorry babes, I didn't know.'

By the time security got there, they were hugging. We stayed for a while and all left together? Me, Clarke, Chrissy, and the couple. We were going back to their place when I snapped out of and bailed back home..

But like I said, I don't really count that one, on account of it literally being rape..

Chapter 6

Pick Up Styx..

I got a call from Jimmy one day, he was heading over to see an old friend from Tamworth, that was staying at his sister's for his birthday. So we went over there for a drink, and his ex was there, with their little girl. I'm on a fucking merry-go-round here I swear. I did always like Stacey, or Styx as they called her. She's hot. But she was always with Scott. However, quite recently, Stacey had left Scott for his best mate Shane. Bit of a shocking revelation really, especially because she had left Shane behind in Tammy. It's complicated much?

Anywho, Scott was super paranoid that I was going to get with Stacey, and kept trying to set me up with his sister. Who he mentioned many times was an ex-prostitute. Whatever dude. I don't like being accused of things I didn't do. It's this thing I have with the truth. Basically, all you are doing is whining about something I haven't done, yet..

Because if you accuse me of it, and act like I've done it, treating me as if I did it.. Well shit, the only ingredient missing, is I may as well go ahead and fucking do it. And I did. After everyone had gone to bed except us, Stacey and I were sitting on the couch talking, and I put my hand in her lap. Her eyes lit up and she said;

'I hoped you wanted to.'

She took that same hand and led me outside and into the garage. After she flipped over a mattress, we fell on top of it and had sex for about three and a half minutes. I whole thing felt rushed, and naughty, and good.

Until we went back inside that is. We were sitting at the table, talking for a while and Scott came back out. Upon seeing him, Stacey immediately jumped a seat over and stopped talking. Red hot. She did it on purpose. Made him cry man. That was fucking cruel, and I felt terrible. I awkwardly slipped outside, back into the garage, and laid on the mattress, staring at the roof until Jimmy woke up and we cut..

Chapter 7

Seventh Heaven..

A bit of a long story short, I had a bit of cash money. So I did what any normal bloke with money does, went into the Valley with me mate Jimmy. We went to the strip joint, which was fucking expensive, no matter how much money you have. Then a couple of other places, met these two chicks at one, couldn't give you any names sorry, of the girls or the clubs. At one of the clubs, not sure which, Jimmy got denied access because he was wearing cargo pants. Fuck off. I think this was our fourth or fifth club and no problems so far. He just didn't like the look of him.

'It's alright. Thanks for everything brother, but I'm gonna take off.'

"Na. Come on man, we'll go somewhere else."

'It's getting late bred. I'll just head home hey and see ya at work.'

In truth, it was early. It was daylight and people were sitting across the road drinking beers and eating waffles. I wanted to go over there so bad but had already paid the cover charge for the three of us, so we just went in. All of a sudden I had two chicks. Nice. Ish. After a while, I couldn't help but notice that the prettier one kept banging on about her ex. Are there no other tunes? So I changed my attack formation. But the other chick whispered in my ear that she can do everything but sex because she just had a pap smear. Major turn on. Bert. Pump the breaks. So I kinda ditched them and went to a brothel..

Actually, that was exactly what I did. Shit, I went from one chick, to two chicks, to no chicks. Fuck it. Not sure what it was called, but when I walked in the madam sat me down, got me a complimentary Jack Daniels, and explained that two girls were working. They would come out, do a little turn, and walk back off. And I was to tell her which one I liked. Cold. But I was in Rome again. I think most blokes have to visit a Brothel as part of their bucket list.

I finished my drink and walked over to let her know I liked the first one with the big bazookas and the fishnet stockings, but then I asked her on the sly which one does more.

"OK, I'd like the second one please."

It was $120 for a halfa or $180 for the full hour. I spun out because that was the same price for a lap dance at the strip club, suckers. She escorted me to the room, pun intended, where my lady for the evening awaited. Well..

First, she got me to come over, under the blue light and told me to pull out my penis and pull the skin back. Very romantic. The "blue light" reveals all kinds of nasties that like to hang around trouser snakes. All clear. Then she told me how it was going down.

I was to have a shower in front of her. Then lay on the bed face down. She was going to give me a short massage, rubbing her tits on my back a little and then we would have sex. She was to put the condom on with her mouth, then only she would put it in, and she repeated that. Told you, a real charmer.

But most of all she emphasized that I was NOT to come inside her. I was to pull out and she would finish the deed by hand. She then added on the sly that kissing on the neck was an extra 50 cash. Dirty Birdy. But not as dirty as I had hoped. I asked a few questions, and got a few no's, all of which are strictly confidential between me and my sex care professional..

So I threw her a pineapple and we did the shower and massage thing. Just as she said, she did the condom thing and the sex stuff. I tried a few different positions, but she got sick of them real quick hey. At one stage she actually said;

'I'm not a fucking gymnast ya know!'

Well, shit lady. Perhaps not, but you are a prostitute, and I did just pay you for this exact reason hey. But whatever, back to church sex if you want, but you guessed it, I did the one thing she told me NOT to do. She knew straight away. Mark of a real pro. Pounced me off her and said;

'You just CAME!!'

I said: "No I didn't."

Haha, "No I didn't?", did I just say, "No I didn't?" ROFL..

Ah man I cracked up writing that. But what happened next was even funnier. She ripped the franger straight off me in a flash and cum spurted everywhere, all over her tits, down her stomach, on her thighs and in her lap. And she had a single drop running down her cheek, that made her look so sad, hooker mime..

'You fuckhead! Now I have to get the fucking morning-after pill. How the fuck could you not know you came?'

I just ran with it. "I don't know, and I just gave you 50 bucks, and the rest, just take it out of that."

She was not impressed. But to be fair, neither was I. So it all worked out in the end..

'Probably all the drugs you've taken tonight. You can't even feel your own dick.'

Ok lady. You're pretty much writing the story now, so I again just ran with it. I wanted to tell her that I did it on purpose so bad, but she might of attacked me. She told me to get dressed and get out. And I told her I was having another shower first. And she really didn't like that, so I took extra care of my nether regions while she eagle-eyed me, dagger style.. I finished up, dried off, got dressed, and took off..

She never even said goodbye..

Chapter 8

Big Bertha..

Not being rude. That's what they call her. Two of the main black families in Ipswich are the Massos, who are mostly blokes, and the Parsons, who are mostly women. Both of whom mostly reside out in Leichhardt, basically the second biggest ghetto in Ipswich. I was staying in a share house at the time when I met this chick Aimee, who was a Parsons, and very cute. I liked her and I could tell she liked me. But I wasn't sure if we were related or not, so I didn't say anything until I asked my Uncle. All good, but she beat me to it.

I was sitting down having dinner one arvo when I could hear her talking to one of the other chicks that lived there.

'You just have to be confident girl! Just go up and ask him.'

What's going on here? And then, she just walked up and asked me;

'What are you doing tonight? Want to come drinking with us?'

"Yea I do. Just let me finish having this chew."

So, the other chick Shae, drove us out to Aimee's cousin's place, stopping in at a bottle-o on the way. It was a pretty quiet drive, as we were both pretty nervous. Except for Shae, who found stirring us hilarious. When we got there, however, Aimee came out of her shell, and I started constructing a second one. There was a group of black women sitting around the kitchen table, having seven loud conversations between the five of them.

I went to sit down and introduce myself, but the lady of the house beat me to it. She was a small woman with a big attitude and sitting at the head of the table.

'I'm Isabella Rockefeller, nice to meet you love, have a seat.'

"Hi, I'm Daniel.' I squeaked, not entirely sure if she was serious or not.

'Mum. Stop being stupid. That's not really her name.', another chick told me.

'Samantha's my name,' but I found out later, they all called her Birtha, 'this is my place. That's Carly, Mary, Anne, Tiffany, and Michelle, you met Mum and I guess you already know Aimee hey?'

"Yea we kinda live together." Even though 'Isabella' was sitting at the head of the table, and doing a damn good job at being the loudest, Bertha was clearly in charge. She was more just letting her mum do as she pleased. But now and then she would chip in and pull her back. After about an hour or so, another sister turned up, with her girlfriend. I was already surrounded, but this really threw a spanner in the mix. The daughter, Lee, was tall and lean, and proud. She had a haircut that said 'yea I'm a lesbian so what!?' while her chick, on the other hand, was a small petite blonde with a mousy stature.

They came in, sat down, and joined in, but things got extremely awkward extremely quick, and not just for me anymore. Lee and Isabella were at each right from the get-go. Didn't matter what the other was talking about, they both had good reasons as to why they should argue over it. Back and forth for about 20 minutes until Lee finally snapped, sprung to her feet, and screamed;

"Mum what's your fucking problem with me? Everything I do! Everything I say! You're always at me! Fucking why?"

'Because you're a fucking p00fter! That's why!' Isabella bounced up and screamed back at her. Lee took her girl's hand and headed for the door.

"Come on babe! We're out of here. We don't have to sit here and take this shit from an ignorant old CUNT LIKE THAT!" She announced, pointing at her mum.

I had no idea what to do, except to remain both quiet and still. It was one of the most uncomfortable experiences of my life. And pretty heartbreaking too. Lee seemed cool, and her girlfriend was sweet as. Her mum on the other hand was a total bitch. Aimee told me not to worry because they were apparently like that all the time. It however did not stop me from worrying. I avoided eye contact with Isabella from then on and only spoke when spoken to. She must of figure I was just a whipped dog, and no fun to play with anymore. However, Aimee came to the same conclusion, and she got dressed up with the majority of the other girls and they took off.

She gave me a look on the way out that said 'Are you coming or not?' and I gave her one back that said "I wanna go home." All of a sudden the house was silent, mostly because Isabella left with them, and now it was only me, Samantha and Tiffany left. Tiffany finished her drink and went to bed in one of the spare rooms, and I decided to call it a night as well.

"Can I use your phone to call a cab please Sam, I left mine at home?"

'No you can't.' she said.

"What? How come?" I asked her, confused.

'If you want to go home, you're gonna have to walk.' Wtf?

"OK. Is it alright if I just crash on the couch here then?"

'No. If you stay here you have to sleep in my bed.'

I see what's going on here. This is extortion. She's blackmailing a black male. All I wanted to do was go to bed. It was getting late and the grog was wearing off. I hadn't been drinking too hard, and there is nothing worse than going from drunk to sober while you are still awake.

"Come on, just let me use the phone, please. Or just sleep on the couch."

'No, I said. You can either come to bed, or you can fuck off walking!'

She got a bit stern about it too. Really though, what was I gonna do? Walk all the way home and turn down sex in the process. Stuff that. So I went to bed with her and it didn't take long before she started feeling up my thigh and kissing on my neck. Turned out I had a good time. For someone that was tired, we sure sexed a lot. Halfway through, during a position change, she asked if she could suck my dick. Haha, sure, I like that..

Later on, while I was back on top, and knew when I was about to come, without a word she latched onto me and made me finish inside her. I passed out for a while but was woken up by her butt, grinding into my groin. We had sex again, went back to sleep, and woke up in the morning. Before getting out of bed, she rode me again then went out to meet the girls, who had all arrived back home and were eagerly awaiting her verdict.

'Holy fuck he's got a big budoo!' She announced loudly. 'I think he tore me!'

Holy fuck alright, how embarrassing, I know heaps of blokes would like that, but it made me want to hide under the blankets. Now I had to leave through a crowd of judging eyes, including Aimee and Shae who were both sitting around the table again. Awkward..

"Hey Shae, you heading home soon? Can I get a lift please?"

'Yea, brother! Whatever you need.' She said with a grimacing grin.

Aimee stayed at Samantha's, probably just because she didn't want to share a ride home with me. Shae wouldn't stop laughing at me as I explained to her what happened. She couldn't understand why I got with Birtha, who was older than me by about 10 years, wasn't as thin or pretty as Aimee, and has a kid. But as I explained it all made sense to her. She then told me about her sisters and some of the things they got up to, and I actually felt a bit better..

After we got home I had a shower and a proper sleep. Two days later when I was having dinner again, Birtha turned up in a taxi, with a stick and a three-rack of XXXX Bitter, my favorite. So I went back with her to her place where she waiting for me to have a sesh and get drunk. And when I was done she took me into the room and ravished me. This went on for nearly two months. Taxi, weed, beer, sex. Taxi, weed, beer, sex. Until one day it went; taxi, weed, beer, sex, I'm pregnant..

"How far along are you?" I asked her.

'3 months. It's yours.'

"Huh? Sam we've only been together for a month and a half. Two max.."

She looked at me so blankly, she fucked up on the maths and now it was too late. I could tell she was lying and knew she just got caught out. I didn't say anything else, just got dressed and walked home. She turned up a couple of days later but I got one of the other blokes to answer the door and say I wasn't home..

Chapter 9

Doing Time..

A short while later I was living in Booval, Ipswich's biggest ghetto, when I ran into a cousin of mine, Mike. He told me he was going drinking around this chick's place and that he would shout me if I tagged along. So I followed him along to a set of flats that definitely looked like they belonged in the ghetto. When we got there, Mary welcomed us in and closed the door behind us. She was a short, stumpy black woman missing at least three teeth, not sure where they were..

I was confused at first, she was flirting with me, talking about her 'man' in jail. but kept grabbing Mike on either the ass or the crouch, depending on which way he was facing. Then it all made sense, she was a slut, and a tease as well. She kept pretending to go down on Mike, but would slap it away and call him disgusting. She was really starting to annoy the both of us. After a while I had enough and told her;

"Either you give him head, or I'm going home, fuck this!"

Reminded myself of Big Bertha barking orders around. But she took him into the room and what felt like about three hours later, they came back out and Mike went home..

Fuck it. I followed her into the room next, and without a word, she took off her pants and sprawled out on the bed. I hopped on top of her and after about thirty seconds she started squirting like a fire hydrant. I'm not gonna lie, even though she wasn't really my type, I found it very hot. Probably because I knew as a fact that I made her cum, I on the other hand couldn't for the life of me. The whole situation had turned me off a bit and I just could get there. I ended up finishing myself off in the shower and went home..

A couple of weeks later her 'man' got out of jail and I ran into him and his son at a mate's place. He knew who I was and what had happened, and let me know he did when he introduced himself. He made a point of staring me too hard in the eye and held onto my hand for a little bit too long. They sat on either side of me and I could tell they were waiting for me to let my guard down, but I never gave them the chance.

After a while, they realized that they weren't going to get a clean shot in and left, haven't seen any of them since..

About a month later, the law caught up with me and it was my turn to go directly to jail. I went two and a half years without even smelling a woman and apparently left my libido in there, because I stayed celibate for another three and a half after that..

Chapter 10

Never Again..

After I got out of jail, I was quiet for a long time. I had just finished doing two and half years and had two and a half more parole. So I kept to myself, apart from when I was at work I didn't really see anyone but the postie. My parole was nearly up when I got an opportunity to go to University and stay on campus at quite a nice college..

When I arrived I felt like a fish out of water, I was clearly 37 years older than everyone else and was treated like a leaper, which I actually didn't mind. I was the only Fresher to miss O' Week, the hazing that went with it, and all the blind dates with random chicks. That's all these guys worried about, about four times a day they were matched up with a different chick from a different college.

After twelve months of studying for a bachelor of arts, I gave up and moved back to Ipswich. Centrelink however must have missed the memo, because they gave me $1000 at the start of the year to buy study materials. So I bought a big chunk of weed and took a Greyhound down to Tamworth and stayed at my Aunties place for a few days while I offloaded it. Weed in Brisbane is about half the price of weed in Tamworth and by selling it in small quantities, I more than doubled my money..

I gave a mate $100, plus food and fuel, to drive me to Ipswich and back, and did it again. And again and again. I stopped selling small stuff and having to deal with the small fries and was making some decent coin. Too much actually, it was just me and my Aunty living there and all she wanted from me was to keep the fridge and cupboards full. I usually spend my spare money on weed, but since I had plenty of weed, I had plenty of spare money. I bought a car and a few other things, but I'm quite easy to please..

At this stage, I was selling only quarters up, which meant a hundred dollar minimum each sale, and I got sick of taking decent money off of people that didn't spend any on their own kids. One day I was taking my new dog to the vet and I had my little cousin Kelly with me. On the way, we passed the old basketball stadium with had been converted into a skating rink.

That weekend I took Kelly and her little brother and sister skating and we all had a blast. I used to go when I was little and forgot just how much fun it is. The following weekend Kelly asked if a couple of her friends could come too. Of course I told her, but made sure my Aunty came along as well. Mainly because I didn't know who the other kids were, and thought their parents might think it was a bit sus. My Aunty is well known and respected in those parts, as every Wednesday the Church holds a free BBQ in her front yard.

So the next weekend came along and there were five kids. The next week there were eight. Fifteen. Twenty-seven. Thirty-four. They were coming out of the woodwork. I didn't mind, they were all welcome. At first I was driving them, then I had to get a Maxi Taxi as well, and then it was just too much logistically, so we all worked there. The whole neighbourhood knew what I was doing and had a tone of good things to say about it, but only one ever chipped in. Kylie. She had four kids who all came skating and would usually hang around for an hour or two afterward playing out the front. One Saturday, her eldest girl came up and gave me $50..

'Mum said to give this to you.'

"Yea cool. Tell her I said thanks heaps hey." I had met Kylie before I started up skating while I was getting about wheeling and dealing. She turned over a little bit of weed every now and then, and most people around knew her. I asked my Aunty about her and she told me that she had a man in jail that was getting out soon..

I went around after skating to thank her and I could see in her eyes straight away that it was a trap. She gave me that money to lure me in and get on my good side, but I'm not that easy so I ignored it, at first lol..

The next weekend she had a boyfriend, a red-headed bloke named Pete, plus her man in jail, who was the father of her kids and expecting her to be there when he got out. It was the talk of the town for a little while, until they broke up, and got back together several times and I guess everyone just got over it..

After around a month of that going on, she turned up with the kids and a birthday cake for my birthday. Caramel mud cake too, my favorite. She'd done her research and was on the hunt;

'You look even more handsome with your beard shaved.' she told me.

"Ah yea, aren't you with Pete though?"

'Na he went back to his ex.'

"And what about your bloke in jail?"

'He's not my bloke, and he's still got a month to go anyways.'

I was in the routine of getting quite drunk and stoned after skating, a little treat for myself I guess. But that arvo I hit it pretty hard, with Kylie on my mind the whole time. Eventually, I walked up to her place and knocked on the door. She lit up when she saw me and told the kids to get ready for bed. We were standing in the hallway as she was directing traffic and I couldn't stop staring at about an inch of skin that was exposed between the top of her jeans and the bottom of her shirt. As I reached out and lightly pinched her hip, she looked me in the eye and sang out over her shoulder;

'Kids. Bed. Now.'

We went into her room and she pulled me on top of her and onto the bed. I hadn't had sex in over six years, but I was thinking about it. In fact, I had a move I thought of, and was waiting to try out. While I was grinding on top of her and chewing on her neck, I slipped my hand down the front of her pants and fingered her in rhythm with the grind, acting as if they were my prick, I call it 'rounding third'. I only got about three or four pumps in when she started ripping off both of our clothes at the same time..

Now I don't know much about poor old Pete, but I can tell you for sure that he has a needle dick. I nearly squeaked when I put it in, she was easily the tightest chick I've ever been with. But I couldn't let her know that, she already thought she had me by the balls. About two minutes later I asked if I could come inside her and she pulled me in with her thighs. I looked at her and could tell she didn't come by the look she was giving me.

"I can go again.."

She lit up again and jumped on top, I pinched some saliva from the tip of my tongue and rubbed it on her clit until she climaxed and I did as well. After we got dressed, she grabbed my number and saved it under 'Michael'..

A few days later, a cousin of mine told me that she had seen Kylie and Pete back together. A few days later she booty called me and came over. It was the first time she had been in my room but made herself very comfortable. After going through my shit, she threw herself on the bed and beckoned me over. As I hopped into bed, my dog who was still a pup at the time and accustomed to jumping into bed with me each night, looked at me, stared Kylie right in the eye, growled, and walk out. Probably should have listened to her hey. I didn't though, Kylie and I hooked up a few times after that. She always seemed to be sneaking around and have some cheesy line up her sleeve..

Well, the day finally came, and her man David got out of jail. He was a short, stocky blonde dude with an IQ of about 7. He moved back in even though she had moved on with another bloke, and was still seeing me on the sly. He didn't have much going on upstairs, but I can tell you now, he had a fat cock. Kylie went from a tight fit to having to work for it. She was a bad bitch hey, playing all three of us. She really got off over all the secrets and the sneaking around..

It had been three weeks since I had seen her, and the only time I didn't get her a morning-after pill, which I was regretting ever since. And rightfully so, she came around one morning with David in tow and was acting weird, making small talk with me and Aunty. She finally got me alone and said;

'I just took a pregnancy test and I'm three weeks.'

"I'm not booking you up." I told her, knowing the type of woman she was, I thought she might have just been working an angle to get credit. She was telling the truth though, and as she started to show, the rumors started to spread. A couple at a time, kids stopped turning up for skating, until one week there were only five. I'd lost my integrity and their trust, getting involved with a woman that was already involved with two other men. She started texting me heaps and I told her that if the kid was mine that I'd do the right thing, and it should be pretty easy to tell because it would either be red, black, or yellow..

The day finally came and she had a little boy, with a full head of red hair, who she named Michael Jack, after the alias she had for me in her phone, and my middle name..

That was over a year ago now, and unless I'm going to the toilet or having a shower, I haven't taken my penis out since..